W9-BIU-810

Big Cats

Lions

by Marie Brandle

Bullfrog
Books

Ideas for Parents and Teachers

Bullfrog Books let children practice reading informational text at the earliest reading levels. Repetition, familiar words, and photo labels support early readers.

Before Reading

- Discuss the cover photo. What does it tell them?

- Look at the picture glossary together. Read and discuss the words.

Read the Book

- "Walk" through the book and look at the photos. Let the child ask questions. Point out the photo labels.

- Read the book to the child, or have him or her read independently.

After Reading

- Prompt the child to think more. Ask: What did you know about lions before reading this book? What more would you like to learn about them?

Bullfrog Books are published by Jump!
5357 Penn Avenue South
Minneapolis, MN 55419
www.jumplibrary.com

Library of Congress Cataloging-in-Publication Data

Names: Brandle, Marie, 1989– author.
Title: Lions / by Marie Brandle.
Description: Minneapolis, MN: Jump!, Inc., [2021]
Series: Big cats | Includes index.
Audience: Ages 5–8 | Audience: Grades K–1
Identifiers: LCCN 2020023426 (print)
LCCN 2020023427 (ebook)
ISBN 9781645277262 (ebook)
ISBN 9781645277255 (hardcover)
Subjects: LCSH: Lion—Juvenile literature.
Classification: LCC QL737.C23 (ebook) | LCC QL737.
C23 B7248 2021 (print) | DDC 599.757—dc23
LC record available at https://lccn.loc.gov/2020023426
LC ebook record available at https://lccn.loc.gov/2020023427

Editor: Eliza Leahy
Designer: Michelle Sonnek

Photo Credits: Eric Isselee/Shutterstock, cover, 1, 3, 17, 24; Simon Dannhauer/Shutterstock, 4, 23tr; Vibrant Image Studio/Shutterstock, 5 (sky); lindsay_imagery/iStock, 5 (lions); Ringadingding/iStock, 6–7, 23br; Lifehunter/iStock, 8–9; imageBROKER/Alamy, 10–11; Carole Deschuymere/Alamy, 12; AfriPics/Alamy, 13, 23bl; Henk Bogaard/iStock, 14–15; Albie Venter/SuperStock, 16, 23tl; John Ceulemans/Shutterstock, 18–19; SuperStock, 20–21.

Printed in the United States of America at Corporate Graphics in North Mankato, Minnesota.

Table of Contents

Life in a Pride

This is Africa.

It is morning in the grasslands.

Lions wake up.
They are big cats.

pride

Lions live in groups.
We call them prides.
How many lions are
in this one?

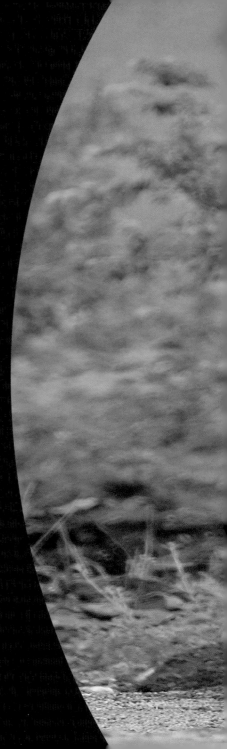

Males guard each pride.
They have big manes.
Roar!

mane

Males from different prides fight.

Why?

They guard their land.

Females hunt in groups.
Their gold fur helps them hide.

They run after prey.

African buffalo

They bring food home.

The pride eats.

Cubs play.
Cute!

cub

Dad plays, too.
They learn to hunt.

17

Lions climb.

They rest in trees.

They sleep a lot.

How much?

Up to 20 hours a day.

Time for a nap!

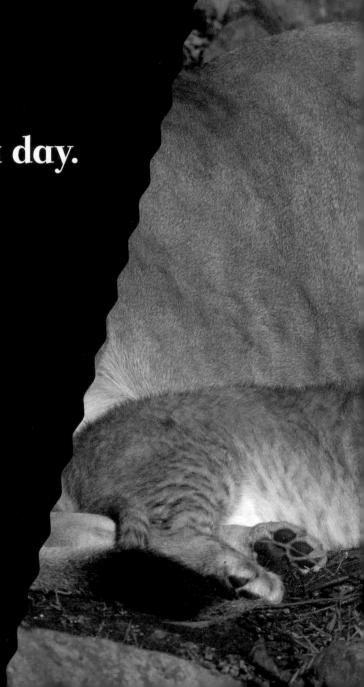

Where in the World?

Most lions live in African grasslands. A small number live in forests in India. Take a look!

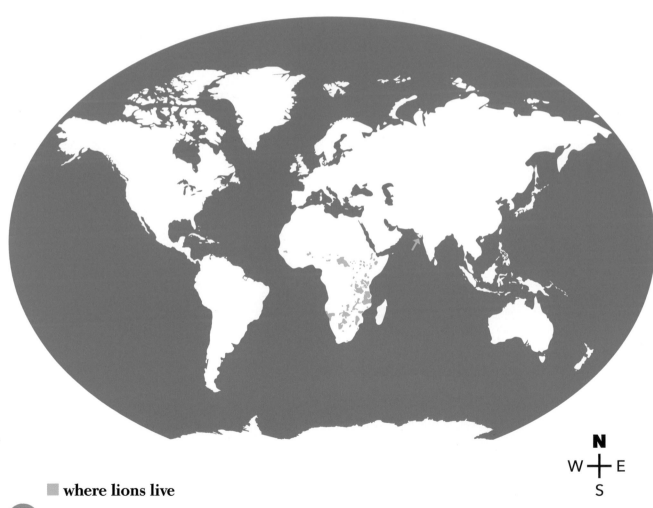

■ where lions live

Picture Glossary

cubs
Young lions.

grasslands
Large, open areas of grass.

prey
Animals that are hunted by other animals for food.

prides
Groups of lions that consist of adult males and females and their cubs.

Index

To Learn More

Finding more information is as easy as 1, 2, 3.

❶ Go to www.factsurfer.com

❷ Enter "lions" into the search box.

❸ Choose your book to see a list of websites.